MEDITATIONS ON THE WAY OF THE CROSS

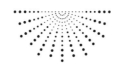

MARY PEZZULO

APOCRYPHILE
PRESS

Apocryphile Press
1700 Shattuck Ave #81
Berkeley, CA 94709
www.apocryphilepress.com

Copyright © 2020 by Mary Pezzulo
Printed in the United States of America
ISBN 978-1-949643-43-5 | paperback
ISBN 978-1-949643-44-2 | epub

All rights reserved. No part of this book may be reproduced, stored in a
retrieval system, or transmitted in any form or by any means— electronic,
mechanical, photocopy, recording, or other- wise— without written
permission of the author and publisher, except for brief quotations in printed
reviews.

Please join our mailing list at www.apocryphilepress.com/free
We'll keep you up-to-date on all our new releases,
and we'll also send you a FREE BOOK.
Visit us today!

CONTENTS

Introduction   V

1. The First Station: Jesus is Condemned to Death   I
2. The Second Station: Jesus Accepts His Cross   5
3. The Third Station: Jesus Falls the First Time   8
4. The Fourth Station: Jesus Meets His Mother   I I
5. The Fifth Station: Simon of Cyrene Helps Jesus   I4
   Carry His Cross
6. The Sixth Station: Veronica Wipes the Face of   I7
   Jesus
7. The Seventh Station: Jesus Falls the Second Time   20
8. The Eighth Station: Jesus Consoles the Women of   23
   Jerusalem
9. The Ninth Station: Jesus Falls the Third Time   26
10. The Tenth Station: Jesus is Stripped of His   29
    Garments
11. The Eleventh Station: Jesus is Nailed to the Cross   32
12. The Twelfth Station: Jesus Dies on the Cross   36
13. The Thirteenth Station: Jesus is Taken Down from   40
    the Cross
14. The Fourteenth Station: Jesus is Laid in the Tomb   44
15. The Fifteenth Station: The Resurrection   47

INTRODUCTION

I began meditating on the Way of the Cross when I went to graduate school. At Franciscan University, there is a beautiful walking Way of the Cross, on a hill near the adoration chapel. I walked that trail, meditating, many times. Later, when I was diagnosed with fibromyalgia and stuck at home most of the time, I found a great deal of consolation on meditating on the Way of the Cross from bed, without walking.

When I started my blog, I wanted to observe Lent by writing down the things that went through my head during those walks, two every week until Easter. I was surprised to find that they were very popular with a wide audience of both Catholics and Protestants —including some people who had never cared for the Way of the Cross devotion before. I saw that the story of Christ's passion was so often related in formal, stuffy language that made it seem irrelevant to people's day-to-day life. People hadn't thought about how Christ came to take up their cross and carry it to Calvary, because no one had pointed it out to them.

I hope that in publishing my own meditations on the Way

of the Cross in the form of a book, I can inspire people to remember that Christ walked that terrible road for them and with them, in their own lives and their own sufferings. And I hope that I can show you that in doing so, Christ triumphed —and in the end, so will you. You will triumph because Christ already triumphed over your cross. The Way of the Cross is a sorrowful prayer but also a joyful one, because of the Resurrection.

The Way of the Cross is often prayed as a group, in the church, during Lent, but I would like to encourage everyone to meditate on it this Lent and throughout the year wherever you find yourselves —in the hospital, traveling, while at school or working, while at home. This is where Christ carries His cross, after all: in us, in our day-to-day lives.

None of these ideas are completely my own, because I wrote them down while praying with the whole church and meditating on images the Church has remarked on for thousands of years. But I hope my meditations on this ancient prayer can help you feel that Christ is present with you in your own journey.

1

THE FIRST STATION: JESUS IS CONDEMNED TO DEATH

*W*e adore You, O Christ, and we bless You, because by Your Holy Cross You have redeemed the world.

Pilate then took Jesus and scourged Him. And the soldiers twisted together a crown of thorns and put it on His head, and put a purple robe on Him; and they began to come up to Him and say, "Hail, King of the Jews!" and to give Him slaps in the face. Pilate came out again and said to them, "Behold, I am bringing Him out to you so that you may know that I find no guilt in Him." Jesus then came out, wearing the crown of thorns and the purple robe. Pilate said to them, "Behold, the Man!" So when the chief priests and the officers saw Him, they cried out saying, "Crucify, crucify!" Pilate said to them, "Take Him yourselves and crucify Him, for I find no guilt in Him." The Jews answered him, "We have a law, and by that law He ought to die because He made Himself out to be the Son of God."

Therefore when Pilate heard this statement, he was even

1

more afraid; and he entered into the Praetorium again and said to Jesus, "Where are You from?" But Jesus gave him no answer. So Pilate said to Him, "You do not speak to me? Do You not know that I have authority to release You, and I have authority to crucify You?" Jesus answered, "You would have no authority over Me, unless it had been given you from above; for this reason he who delivered Me to you has the greater sin." As a result of this Pilate made efforts to release Him, but the Jews cried out saying, "If you release this Man, you are no friend of Caesar; everyone who makes himself out to be a king opposes Caesar."

Therefore when Pilate heard these words, he brought Jesus out, and sat down on the judgment seat at a place called The Pavement, but in Hebrew, Gabbatha. Now it was the day of preparation for the Passover; it was about the sixth hour. And he said to the Jews, "Behold, your King!" So they cried out, "Away with Him, away with Him, crucify Him!" Pilate said to them, "Shall I crucify your King?" The chief priests answered, "We have no king but Caesar."

So he then handed Him over to them to be crucified.

— JOHN 19:1-16

Behold the Man.

Behold Man.

Behold the source of Man's life.

Behold the Lover of Mankind, in flesh, walking among us, bearing our shame.

John the Forerunner was a prophet. When he saw Christ, he said, "Behold the Lamb of God!"

Pontius Pilate is no prophet. Pilate sees Christ and says, "Behold the Man."

John the Forerunner knew himself to be unworthy to

undo Christ's sandal strap. "I need to be baptized by You, and do You come to me?"

Pilate does not see himself as unworthy. Pilate sees no need for baptism; if it were offered, he would refuse. He does not question why the Lord has come to him. He strips off all the Lord's clothes. He has the Lord scourged. Whatever anyone does to the least among us, they do to Christ. So this is surely not the first time Pilate has beheld Christ and had Him scourged. It may be the thousandth time, for all we know. Scourging Christ is what Pilate does.

Christ went down into the Jordan to be baptized, and all the waters of the world were purified for baptism. Everyone who comes to the water receives healing and forgiveness of sin. But that was years ago, and there is no water flowing now. The waters have turned to blood. Blood is pouring from Christ's wounds; blood smears everyone who touches Him, rendering them unclean before the Old Law. Blood runs over the floor of the Praetorium. Blood stains the judgment seat. Blood soaks into the purple robe, rendering it filthy and useless as a garment; blood flows over the sharp thorns of the crown. Every symbol of kingship and judgment has been eternally stained.

Jesus could have given up the Ghost then, and no one would have been surprised. Plenty of scourging victims died. It happened all the time. But He chooses to stay alive. He is determined to be one with His beloved— with me, with you, with all of us, even with Pilate and the angry crowd who cried for His execution. All of us will someday stand before Christ the Judge. Now Jesus stays alive, so that He may be judged by His beloved and have all things in common with us.

John the Forerunner asked Christ, "Are You the One who is to come? Or shall we look for another?"

John the Forerunner received an answer. "The blind

receive sight and the lame walk, the lepers are cleansed and the deaf hear, the dead are raised up, and the poor have the gospel preached to them. And blessed is he who does not take offense at Me."

Pilate doesn't want to talk about prophecy. Pilate doesn't want to know what is to come; he asks about the past. "Where are you from?"

And Pilate receives no answer. The Kingdom of Heaven is not of this world. Christ's own people sold and abandoned Him. As long as He walks on this earth, He is from nowhere. There is nothing to say.

Pilate asks the people, "Shall I crucify your King?"

The people betray Christ one more time. "We have no King but Caesar."

Blasphemy. The chosen people of God see God, clothed in purple and wearing a crown, and reject Him, preferring Caesar. Caesar despises them and Christ loves them. Caesar enslaves them and Christ promises to set them free. Caesar will destroy their temple within their lifetime; Christ is the God they have invoked on the temple mount for a thousand years. Before Abraham came to be, He Is. But the descendants of Abraham choose Caesar. And so do we. We all have. We've all committed this blasphemy before. Every sin is a choice for Caesar, rather than for Christ.

Jesus submits Himself to His beloved.

His beloved is you.

Let us go out to Golgotha with Him.

Let us go to the Wedding Feast of the Lamb.

Behold, the Lamb of God.

Behold, your lover.

Behold, the Man.

THE SECOND STATION: JESUS ACCEPTS HIS CROSS

*W*e adore you, O Christ, and we bless you, because by Your holy cross you have redeemed the world.

Then he handed him over to them to be crucified. So they took Jesus; and carrying the cross by himself, he went out to what is called The Place of the Skull, which in Hebrew is called Golgotha.

— JOHN 19:17

God is God, and can do whatever He wills. He said "Let there be light," and there was light, days before the stars existed to contain the light. Such was His will and pleasure.

Now, He takes up a cross, and carries it Himself.

Why does He take up the cross?

It must be because He wills it. No one can force Him to do something He does not will. When Herod tried to kill

Him, He fled with His parents into Egypt and was safe. When the villagers tried to hurl Him off a cliff, He passed through their midst unharmed. When they picked up rocks to stone Him, He left in safety. He could leave at any moment.

Why does He stay?

Why does He carry the cross Himself?

Because it is yours, and He loves you.

This is the wedding custom of Heaven. First, the Bridegroom takes everything the bride has to Himself; then He pours Himself out on the bride. And so it is today. The Wedding Feast of the Lamb has begun. It begins in the Passion and will culminate in Heaven. In Heaven, He will give to you, His bride, every good gift. But first, He takes everything that is yours upon Himself. You long for Heaven, but you don't live in Heaven, so He came down from Heaven to be with you. You are in pain, and He willingly accepts pain. You have weakness, and He takes that as well. You have humiliation, fear, sorrow, failure, loneliness, despair. Your Bridegroom comes to you, crowned with your crown of thorns, covered with your welts, tortured to the point of death because death and torture are the currency of this fallen world. He picks up your dowry, everything you have, and He carries it to Golgotha to be nailed to it, and die your death.

There is nowhere that you can go, where He has not been. There is no suffering that can befall you, which He will not suffer with you. You will find Him in poverty. You will find Him in slavery. He is present in war, in sickness, in despair. If anyone abuses you, they abuse Christ. If anyone abandons you, they abandon Christ. If they rape you or murder you, they do the same to Him.

Somehow, someday, all will be made well, through the mercy of God. He will wipe every tear from our eyes on that day.

But first come Good Friday and the Cross. First, the terrible Mystery: that whenever we cry tears, our God cries with us. And whenever we are broken, Christ is broken with us. And whenever our burdens are too heavy to bear, the Lover of Mankind is there, in the overwhelm, overwhelmed, suffering as we suffer.

The Wedding Feast of the Lamb has begun.

Go and give everything you have to Him.

Let Him carry it to Golgotha with you.

3

THE THIRD STATION: JESUS FALLS THE FIRST TIME

*W*e adore You, O Christ, and we bless You, because by Your holy Cross you have redeemed the world.

Surely he took up our pain
and bore our suffering,
yet we considered him punished by God,
stricken by him, and afflicted.
But he was pierced for our transgressions,
he was crushed for our iniquities;
the punishment that brought us peace was on him,
and by his wounds we are healed.
We all, like sheep, have gone astray,
each of us has turned to our own way;
and the Lord has laid on him
the iniquity of us all.
He was oppressed and afflicted,
yet he did not open his mouth;
he was led like a lamb to the slaughter,

and as a sheep before its shearers is silent,
so he did not open his mouth.

— ISAIAH 53:4-7

He has fallen.

The Son of God has fallen.

The Lover of Mankind has fallen under His cross.

He came down from Heaven to Earth in order to take you to Himself; now He goes lower, and falls on the ground where you lie. The guards are impatient. There is a long walk out to the place of execution in the heat of the desert sun. They want to get it over with, but their prisoner is too weak. They are whipping Him, kicking Him, pulling His torn and bleeding arms, yanking on the robe that sticks to the scourge wounds on His back. They are angry.

God has fallen, and Man is angry with Him for His weakness.

This is our King, in Whom lies all of our hope.

If you are a Christian, you worship a God who fell– not a God who knows, intellectually, what it's like to fall, but a God who fell. You worship a God who was exhausted, ruined, regarded as nothing and cast into the street. You worship a God who had scourges on His back and arms. A God who was ugly. A God who made a fool of Himself. A God who deliberately created an object so heavy that He couldn't carry it. He picked it up anyway, and fell under its weight, and His children whom He loved were angry with Him.

Why would God do such a thing?

He did this out of love, to transform and redeem your fall.

He fell, so that falls might be redeemed.

Our God fell, so that a fall might become a thing of God.

From Good Friday until the end of time, the meaning of a fall has been redeemed. Failure itself has been sanctified. When you see someone who is ruined, broken, fallen, destroyed– when you see a failure, an embarrassment, someone who is less than worthless in the sight of the world– you see an icon of the God who fell. Everyone who helps those whom the world regards as failures, does as much for the God who fell.

Whatever you attempt, in all of your life, when you fail– and you will fail, all human beings fail– you become a sign for the whole world– a sign of the Cross, a sign of the God who fell.

God falls with you. God will revive you, if you take hold of Him; he will rise, and take you with Him to Calvary.

All human beings go to Calvary. There's no avoiding it. Calvary is the end of life, and all life ends in this fallen world.

But we who reverence the God who fell will find, through Calvary, the way Home.

4

THE FOURTH STATION: JESUS MEETS HIS MOTHER

*W*e adore You, O Christ, and we bless You, because by Your holy cross you have redeemed the world.

Is it nothing to you, all you that pass by? behold, and see if there be any sorrow like to my sorrow, which is done to me, with which the LORD has afflicted me in the day of his fierce anger.

— LAMENTATIONS 1:12

She has been here all along.

This was the fulfillment of Simeon's prophecy; this was the sword that ran through her heart. She watches— she could not stop it from coming to this, and she cannot make it better. She watched her only Son betrayed, mocked, tortured to the point of death and sentenced to execution anyway; now she watches Him dragged out to die. The angel told her of His coming, but the angels are silent now. She saw Him worshiped by shepherds; now she sees Him led like a lamb to the slaughter. She welcomed the Magi who came to honor Him; now she sees Him crowned with thorns and led away. She saw Him heal the blind and the leper, but now His own blood is blinding Him and He is torn apart, more hideous to behold than any leper.

She rejoiced to find Him in the temple, and now she is losing Him again.

There is nothing she can do but be present, but follow Him until the end.

And so she is.

And now He sees her.

After all these hours of agony, abandoned by His friends, He sees her.

He sees someone who loves Him and has not abandoned Him.

I can't imagine what passes through His mind. Sorrow at her pain, certainly, deeper sorrow than I can comprehend. Those who love perfectly, feel sorrow more deeply than anyone else. But He must have also felt relief, even joy — because those who love perfectly rejoice in love more deeply than anything else, and His mother's love for Him is perfect.

Here is perfect love, from a perfect mother.

Here is our example, for every act of love.

The first act of love is to be present.

Everything else flows from that.

If you love someone, be present to them. Don't shy away from their suffering. Suffer with them. Remain with them when they are betrayed. Stay present when they are ugly; when the whole world mocks their ugliness. Stay present even when there's nothing you can do. Share in their help-lessness. Share in their loneliness. Let those who count them as nothing count you as nothing as well.

The first act of worship is the same.

Worship the wounded Christ the way His mother did.

Follow Him.

Follow close by, no matter what happens. Follow even though you don't think you do Him any service. Follow even though the crowd is thick and loud, and you think there's no way you'll be seen. Remain close by Him when He doesn't seem like God or even a king anymore. Remain even when the very signs of kingship look like mockery and farce. Remain and Christ will see you.

He will look at you.

The Lover of Mankind will look at you, and be glad that you are there.

5

THE FIFTH STATION: SIMON OF CYRENE HELPS JESUS CARRY HIS CROSS

*W*e adore you, O Christ, and we bless You, because by Your holy cross You have redeemed the world.

As they led him away, they seized a man, Simon of Cyrene, who was coming from the country, and they laid the cross on him, and made him carry it behind Jesus.

— LUKE 23:26

He can't go on. He is exhausted. No amount of pulling, pushing, flogging and screaming will make Him. He is too weak, and in too much pain. The guards can't make Him carry that cross all the way to Calvary. He'll never last that long. They won't get to have their fun if He isn't helped, but the guards don't want to help.

The Lover of Mankind has become a burden.

There is a law that a Roman can press a foreigner into

service, to carry a burden for one mile. Here is a foreigner, Simon of Cyrene. The Romans press him into service, to carry the cross with Jesus.

Simon doesn't know that he's been pressed into carrying the ciborium; he doesn't know he's taking part in the fulfillment of the Old Covenant, the wedding feast of the King's Son, the sacrifice of God to God. The guards don't know it either. One of them could have picked up the cross, and we'd know their name for all generations, just as we know Simon's. But they didn't pick it up. They pressed Simon into service, and Simon will be remembered as the one who helped Christ.

Now, Christ knows the agony of being a burden. Now, everyone who's ever been thought of or treated as a burden, or felt themselves to be a burden, is one with Christ. Now everyone who needs help to bear her cross, is one with Christ. Now the disabled, the sick, the elderly, children and the dying, are made into a new kind of icon. They were created in the image of God, and are icons of God, but from this day throughout eternity they are also icons of the suffering Christ, who needed help to bear His cross.

If you have been helpless, you are one with Him. If you've felt like a burden to someone you love, so has He. If you have been neglected or abused by your caregiver, you have suffered with Christ. If you know what it's like for the trauma of sickness to be compounded by the trauma of abuse or neglect, the King knows it as well. If the ones who helped you have done so grudgingly, not knowing that you were an icon —Christ's Heart broke with yours. It was Christ they hurt. He will take your suffering to the Cross with His own, and return it to you as glory in the end.

The Father looks at the stairs you couldn't climb, the line you couldn't stand in, the job you couldn't do, and sees the Way of the Cross.

The Heavenly Father looks at those who failed to help and those who helped grudgingly, those who abused you and those who ignored you, and sees the guards who pressed a foreigner into carrying the cross to Calvary, to murder the Son of God.

The King of Heaven looks at the house you don't get to leave because people forget to take you along with them, at your room nobody visits because they have forgotten you. And all He can see is the Ciborium and the Cross.

He looks at you and sees His son.

When this is over, when you go before the Throne of Glory, He will show your via dolorosa to the whole world. Everyone will understand what you endured. Everyone who saw you as a burden will see that you were Christ. And the Father will give you His Son's crown and the highest place, because Christ took your passion as His own.

6

THE SIXTH STATION: VERONICA
WIPES THE FACE OF JESUS

$\mathcal{W}$e adore you, O Christ, and we bless You, because by Your holy cross, You have redeemed the world.

He had no beauty or majesty to attract us to him,
nothing in his appearance that we should desire him.
He was despised and rejected by mankind,
a man of suffering, and familiar with pain.
Like one from whom people hide their faces
he was despised, and we held him in low esteem.

— ISAIAH 53:3

It's hard for her to say what he looks like.

Maybe He was never physically beautiful, but He is certainly not now.

His whole body is ugly, crisscrossed by scourge marks, a patchwork of bruises and matted blood. She can barely tell that He's a man —beyond that, she can see that He is ugly, and that He is in pain.

We don't know who this woman is. We don't know her name —"Veronica" means "true icon" and refers to her veil, not to her. We don't know how long she's been following Jesus. There's nothing about her in the Bible, specifically. It could be that she never saw Him before this moment. It could be that she has no idea who He is or what was said about Him.

Somehow she got through the crowd and the guards. Why? Why take that risk?

Why did she run toward Him when His disciples betrayed Him; when His friends denied Him and ran away?

I suppose we'll never know, but here she is.

She takes off her veil, and wipes the blood and dirt from His face.

His eyes are clear, for a moment. For a moment He can see. He looks at her, at the one who had compassion on Him but was helpless to stop His pain. He looks at the one who had nothing to give Him, but came forward anyway, desperate for the chance to help. Compassion Himself gazes upon a compassionate soul.

Then the guards push Him forward to Calvary, leaving the woman behind.His face is forever printed on her veil.

It could be that she didn't know whose face it was, but it was a human face, and she had wiped it clean for a moment. Such a useless gesture, in the grand scheme of things. In a moment the blood would all run back into His eyes. He would fall again at any minute; dust would stick to the blood, and He would be blind and ugly again. And whether He could see or not, He was going to die. He was going to die in agony, with no one to help Him. She couldn't stop any of that.

What she could do, just then, was wipe the blood from His face.

Just then, His suffering was lessened a little.

Just then, He could see compassion.

There is so little we can do, so much of the time. Everyone around us is dying; everyone is hurting. This is the human condition: one long and painful road to Calvary.

But we are called to compassion. Each one of us can help someone, a little, for a moment. Every day there are opportunities to make somebody's road to Calvary easier for a little while, if only we would notice them. If we could have compassion for the condemned men and women all around us, we could be their Veronica. We could make their path easier for a moment, and we could do it again and again for all we meet along our own via dolorosa until we are all in Heaven together.

If we will be faithful to small acts of compassion, Christ will imprint His Countenance on us. Because it is always Christ to Whom we show compassion.

All we have to do is attend Him whenever we see Him passing by on the Way of the Cross.

THE SEVENTH STATION: JESUS FALLS THE SECOND TIME

We adore you, O Christ, and we bless You, because by Your holy cross, you have redeemed the world.

I am poured out like water,
> *and all my bones are out of joint.*
My heart has turned to wax;
> *it has melted within me.*
My mouth is dried up like a potsherd,
> *and my tongue sticks to the roof of my mouth;*
> *you lay me in the dust of death.*

— PSALM 22:14

He has fallen again. The cross weighs down on Him, smashing Him into the dust like a crushed insect. Dust sticks to the blood on His face; it stings His eyes and tickles His parched mouth. He cannot breathe. He can barely move.

A moment ago, Simon was pressed into service to help Him. Veronica only just wiped His face so He could see. Now, a moment later, He's fallen again.

God has fallen, in spite of all our help.

The Prosperity Gospel in all of its forms has been proven a lie. Everyone who tells you that you can earn comfort and success in this earthly life by doing the right thing, should stand dumbstruck before this Mystery. Here is God Himself, Who has never in His life done anything wrong, struggling like an insect face-down in the dirt.

Here is God, useless.

Here is God, helpless.

Here is God, out of breath.

Here is God, Who cannot stand.

Love for you brought Him this low. Pure love and nothing else brought Him to the ground. Love for you brought Him from Heaven to Earth. Love for you brought Him to judgment before Caiaphas, Herod and Pilate. Love for you made Him take up the cross and love for you makes Him lie there, under it, kissing the dirt —because the dirt is where you are.

He wanted you to know that when you are useless, helpless, worn out and unable to stand, that is not your fault. When you can't get back on your feet in spite of the best help, He doesn't think the less of you. When your cross smashes you like an insect, there He is, breathless, smashed, worthless, lying in the dirt with you.

This is the Glory of Heaven, revealed before our eyes —not that the children of God will have worldly success, but that in our misery, we will find the Lord. Our Lord is not an idol made of clay —He is God and Man, a Man whose blood turns the dust to clay to heal our blindness. He is not a help-

21

less idol propped up by human hands, but a helpless Person who fell despite human attempts to help Him. Our God is the Living God, dying before our eyes —dying in us, that we may not die alone. His blood flows into the soil, and the soil is forever sanctified. From now until eternity, anyone who falls on the ground falls onto Christ. Anyone who is blinded by dust is anointed by Christ so that his eyes may be opened. Anyone who drinks sand when he longs for water, drinks the Blood of Christ. Our suffering and our brokenness are one with the suffering and brokenness of Christ.

He could have given up the Ghost right there– He surely wanted to. But this is not the place for Him to die. This is not the hill that God appointed for the redemption of the world. This is not the place of execution chosen for Him by Pilate. Now is not the Hour of Mercy; that's a few hours away. Somehow, His love for you gives Him strength.

With the thought of you before His eyes, He stands.

He goes forward, carrying your cross to Calvary.

THE EIGHTH STATION: JESUS CONSOLES THE WOMEN OF JERUSALEM

𝒲e adore You, O Christ, and we bless, You, because by Your holy cross you have redeemed the world.

A great number of people followed Him, including women who kept mourning and wailing for Him. But Jesus turned to them and said, "Daughters of Jerusalem, do not weep for Me, but weep for yourselves and for your children. Look, the days are coming when people will say, "Blessed are the barren women, the wombs that never bore, and breasts that never nursed." At that time, they will say to the mountains, "fall on us," and to the hills, "cover us." For if men do these things while the tree is green, what will happen when it is dry?"

— LUKE 23:27-31

What consolation is this?

Why would anyone refer to this station as "Jesus Consoles the Women of Jerusalem?"

It sounds like something out of a nightmare. Here is a Man, beaten to the point of death, bleeding out, his head covered in a cap of inch-long thorns, dragging a cross out to his own lynching. You're so terrified, you start to cry, and then he turns to you.

"Do not weep for Me, but weep for yourselves and for your children."

At that point, you'd expect to wake up screaming, but you don't, because it's real. And they drag the Man away and kill Him, leaving you to wonder what he meant.

"Do not weep for Me, but weep for yourselves and for your children. Look, the days are coming when people will say, 'Blessed are the barren women, the wombs that never bore, and breasts that never nursed.'"

Those days are already here, aren't they?

To be a mother is dreadful. Not dreadful as in very bad, but dreadful as in something that fills you with dread. The baby comes to you in an agony of blood and pain. Then your heart is torn open with impossible love, and you know you'd do anything to make them safe and well. You have to make them safe and well. Your whole body and soul are irrevocably changed and you must, whatever the consequences, make your child safe and well.

But you can't.

No mother can make her child safe and well. We live in a fallen world, in an accursed time where mothers cannot make their children safe or well. We live in a world where mothers must take their children and hide in the basement from bombings; where children are afraid to go to sleep, because night is when the explosions begin. Mothers take their children and fly to the border for safety, but they find no solace, only a prison. Mothers take their children onto rafts to flee for their lives, and the children drown. Children are taken away and raped, jailed, tortured, forced into combat, sold into slavery. Children starve to death.

And this horror comes to every mother. No matter how rich or safe or healthy you are, the day will come when your children suffer and you can't make it stop. Not even a perfect mother can make it stop.

Someday, your child will die, and you won't be able to make it stop. I'm trembling with dread as I type these words right now, but I know it's true. Death comes to every human being, and I can't make it stop. Not if I hid in the deepest recesses of the earth —not even if I said to the mountains, "fall on us," and to the hills, "cover us." No mother can make it stop.

Not even the Mother of God could make it stop.

When the wood was green, Herod sent his soldiers to massacre the children of Bethlehem; the Mother of God took her Son and fled into Egypt. Now that the wood is dry, her Child stumbles under its weight, all the way to Calvary, and no one can make it stop.

Now it is the Son of God who is bleeding and in agony. He has watched His beloved sons and daughters suffer and die from the beginning of time, and He will watch them until suffering and death are no more. Today, He is in labor with the New Creation. His heart will be torn open, to make His children safe and well.

Perhaps that's the consolation —the terrible, dreadful consolation to the women of Jerusalem. The Son of God knows what it is to be a mother.

9

THE NINTH STATION: JESUS FALLS
THE THIRD TIME

 e adore You, O Christ, and we bless You, because by Your holy cross You have redeemed the world.

But when I stumbled, they gathered in glee;
   assailants gathered against me without my knowledge.
   They slandered me without ceasing.
   Like the ungodly they maliciously mocked;
   they gnashed their teeth at me.

— PSALM 31:15-18

He is exhausted.

Do you know what it is, to be exhausted? Not merely extremely tired, but exhausted?

To be exhausted is to have nothing left.

He can't walk or crawl. He can't lift His head. He can't open His eyes. Even breathing is difficult.

He is in despair —not the sin of despair, for He never sinned, but the feeling of despair, the feeling that God has abandoned Him and all strength is gone.

And the worst is yet to come.

The guards are dragging Him, but He cannot move. There is nothing left. Not even enough blood in His body. In a minute more, they'll be dragging a corpse.

But then, He thinks of you.

You, personally.

He thinks of you, and how beautiful you are. How remembers how much He has longed to be one with you, since the beginning of time.

He remembers how much pain you are in, and how lonely you feel. He remembers how many times you've felt like a failure and a curse. He thinks back on when all the trouble started, when life began to go wrong, when you discovered you weren't powerful and began to think you weren't worthy of love. He calls to mind the abuse, the depression, the rape, the sickness, the poverty. He recalls when you first felt that He had abandoned you, and how long that feeling has gone on since then.

He thinks of how happy He can make you in Paradise, and how much consolation He can give you with His presence in this life. He could do all of this for you with a single word — He is God, Who created the Heavens and the earth with a word. But there is an even greater act of love He can perform for you.

He can take your suffering onto Himself. He can bring it to the cross. He can lay His body down on the wood, so that when you are nailed to your cross you will be consummating your marriage to the King of Kings. He can be lifted up like the brass serpent in the desert, so that the very symbol of infamy, torture and death will become a symbol of triumph. He can descend into Hell with your pain, so that even if you walk through the valley of the shadow of death, you will know that Christ is present there. He can rise up to Heaven with nail marks pierced all the way through His undying body, so that every time the Father sees a suffering body, He will see His Beloved Son.

He has no physical or emotional strength left; that departed Him when He fell the third time. But He has love for you. No torture or injury could ever destroy that. Not even death can take it away. His love is all that brings Him to His feet. His love drags Him forward when the guards cannot.

The King is enthralled by your beauty and totally in love. In this love, He finishes the journey to Calvary.

THE TENTH STATION: JESUS IS STRIPPED OF HIS GARMENTS

*W*e adore You, O Christ, and we bless You, because by Your holy cross You have redeemed the world.

When the soldiers had crucified Jesus, they took his clothes and divided them into four parts, one for each soldier. They also took his tunic; now the tunic was seamless, woven in one piece from the top.

— JOHN 19:23

We were told the Bridegroom would come at an hour we knew not. It turns out that the hour is a little before Noon, the day before Sabbath during the Passover, when Israel was the property of Rome.

Here is the Bridegroom. You can tell it is He, because He is holding your dowry. Everything that you own is His — your weakness, your pain, your shame, your ugliness. Your crown of humiliation is on His head, and your stripes cover His body. He has taken everything that is yours to Himself — except for your death. That will happen a few hours from now.

You will see the Bridegroom coming again, at another hour and day you don't expect, bringing with Him everything that is His to give to you —happiness, freedom, wisdom, beauty, strength —for the wedding feast that has no end. But first, He takes all that is yours onto Himself.

First, He consummates His marriage with you.

It was always going to be this way. No matter what choices human beings made, God intended that the Son should dwell among us and share our chalice. What was in the chalice, was ours to decide. What have we put in the chalice? Conquest, oppression, mockery, torture, murder, cruelty that calls itself strength. This is how humans treat one another. Christ came into the world to be treated the way His beloved is treated —He volunteered to be born in a conquered nation, to an oppressed race; to be mocked, tortured and murdered by cruel men who believe themselves strong. Because that is the cup His beloved will have to drink. That is your chalice.

This is the Wedding Feast of the Lamb. Your bridegroom is going to drink the wine with you, and consummate your marriage.

They give Him wine mingled with gall, because everything you've had to drink on this fallen world has been mingled with gall. He tastes it, but He does not drink enough that it will interfere with sharing in your pain.

They strip off His robe, re-opening all of His wounds. You wouldn't think He could bleed anymore than He already has, but He is bleeding right now.

Here is God, the Lover of Mankind, Alpha and Omega, Wonderful-Counselor, Father-Forever, King of Kings and Lord of Lords, totally naked for all the world to see.

No, don't look away.

Forget your sense of decency.

Forget your people and your father's house.

Forget where you've come from; forget the weary way of the Cross you have been walking all your life.

The Lord is doing something new. The Wedding Feast of the Lamb has begun. The Father sent His servants to bring you to the banquet. Perhaps you didn't know you were the bride, but you are. You are the bride of Christ. Everything you've seen Him suffer has been for you. Everything He still has to suffer, is for you. Every joy and glory He will have when He returns to His Father's kingdom, He will share with you, after the marriage is consummated.

Out of love for you, Eternity came to dwell in time, and pitch His tent among men. Now here He is at the Wedding Feast, stripped bare for all the world to see.

THE ELEVENTH STATION: JESUS IS NAILED TO THE CROSS

*C*e Adore You, O Christ, and we bless You, because by Your holy cross you have redeemed the world.

When they came to the place called The Skull, they crucified Him there, along with the criminals, one on His right and the other on His left. Then Jesus said, "Father, forgive them, for they do not know what they are doing."

— LUKE 23:33-34

The pain is beyond all telling.

This is the worst punishment the Romans had ever devised, and they'd thought of many grisly punishments. This is worse than anything the people of Israel ever thought to do to anyone. Their law has stipulations about when an executed corpse could be hung on a tree, but it was the Romans who thought of nailing a live man to a tree, and leaving him there in shame and torment until his own exhaustion suffocated him.

Rome and Israel, the Pagans and the Jews, the unclean and the clean, the modern and the ancient —they conspired together to do the worst thing they could imagine, to an innocent Man. They knew He was innocent. Everyone knew. The Jews could find no consistent testimony against Him. Pilate found no fault in Him. But Israel demanded His execution, and Rome obliged. His own disciples betrayed Him; the rest of His followers deserted Him; one denied even knowing Him three times before dawn.

Except for the Mother of God, there is not a soul in the entire world who is innocent of His death.

This is, after all, what human beings do to God. We see Him, and we can't understand Him, so we try to make Him fit. We try to make Him conform. When He doesn't conform, we get angry. We force Him down onto things we can understand, material things, man-made things like wooden planks. We force His feet one on top of the other so He can't walk any closer. We stretch out His arms so He can't wrap them around us. We find that His wrists don't quite reach as far as we'd like, so we pull on them until they're dislocated. We fear that He might get up, so we take other material things — things we've smelted and molded and sharpened to a nice utilitarian point —and we drive them through His flesh and bone until we've satisfied ourselves that He cannot move.

Here is our handiwork. The all-powerful Creator, naked, scourged, bones exposed, gushing blood, pinned to man-made things by man-made things, helpless. Nice and neat. We're free to look upon Him now, and feel satisfied with ourselves. God looks like something we can understand.

And what does God do? God, who cannot but act justly? The One who can neither deceive nor be deceived, but always does right? What does He do?

He prays.

"Father, forgive them, for they do not know what they are doing."

A plea from God to God, from God suffering to God in paradise, from God in flesh, despised by all, to God enthroned in radiant majesty. One God who cannot be divided, praying, the Son to the Father for mercy on the little ones who do not know what they are doing —on Israel, who should have known, and on Rome, who couldn't have known. Mercy on the ones who know they are children of Abraham but don't act as though they are, and mercy on the ones who never knew Abraham in the first place. Mercy on the children who have broken the Law too many times to remember, and mercy on the ones who never knew the Law. Mercy on the Pharisees, the Sadducees, the scribes, Pilate, the Roman soldiers. Mercy on the Simon who betrayed Him three times and mercy on the Simon who could not keep Him from falling under the cross three times. Mercy on all the world.

They don't know what they're doing.

They ought to know.

But they're so accustomed to crucifying God between man-made things, they can't see what they're doing anymore.

And we do the same.

For all the times we have ignored the call of God to love as He loves, because we thought we knew better, Father, forgive us. For all the times we abused You when You came to us disguised as our neighbor, Christ, forgive us.

For every time we would not give you food or drink because we judged You lazy and undeserving, forgive us. For every time we saw You naked and did not clothe You but judged You scandalous, forgive us. For every time we saw You homeless and did not shelter You because we judged You dangerous, forgive us. For every time we saw You sick and did not visit You but judged You attention-seeking, forgive us. For every time we saw You imprisoned and did not visit You because we judged You deserving of punishment, forgive us. For every time we saw You dead and did not mourn or pray for You because we judged You were none of our business, forgive us.

We ought to have known what we were doing, but we did not. Forgive us.

Father, forgive us.

And He does.

THE TWELFTH STATION: JESUS DIES ON THE CROSS

*W*e adore You, O Christ, and we bless You, because by Your Holy Cross You have redeemed the world.

The people stood by and watched; the rulers, meanwhile, sneered at him and said, "He saved others, let him save himself if he is the chosen one, the Messiah of God." Even the soldiers jeered at him. As they approached to offer him wine they called out, "If you are King of the Jews, save yourself." Above him there was an inscription that read, "This is the King of the Jews."

Now one of the criminals hanging there reviled Jesus, saying, "Are you not the Messiah? Save yourself and us." The other, however, rebuking him, said in reply, "Have you no fear of God, for you are subject to the same condemnation? And indeed, we have been condemned justly, for the sentence we received corresponds to our crimes, but this man has done nothing criminal." Then he said, "Jesus, remember me when you come into your kingdom." He replied to him, "Amen, I say to you, today you will be with me in Paradise."

It was now about noon and darkness came over the whole land until three in the afternoon because of an eclipse of the sun. Then the veil of the temple was torn down the middle. Jesus cried out in a loud voice, "Father, into your hands I commend my spirit"; and when he had said this he breathed his last.

— LUKE 23:32-43

It has finally come to this.

Every prophecy, every covenant, every promise has pointed to this. All of our terrible history began with a tree; now, all of our history has led us to a tree.

By a tree we were destroyed. Our Father tried to warn us. That tree would give us the knowledge of good and evil — because, to know evil, you have to experience evil. And our Father didn't want us to experience evil. He wanted us to be happy. But we had to see for ourselves. Our Father told us that if evil came into the world, we would surely die, but we had to find out what that meant. So we did evil, and became evil, and evil came upon us, and Man became a thing that turned from God to a tree and died. Christ desired to be one with us, wherever we would go. So, with the Father's blessing, He left His Father's house. He came down from Heaven. He permitted evil to befall Himself, He embraced the tree, and He died.

That tree, long ago, was beautiful, green and covered in sweet fruits. The tree we see now is ugly — it bears no leaves or blossoms. Only one fruit hangs there, the fruit of our sin: the Son of God who loves us, disfigured, ruined, crying out in torment and giving up the Ghost. But those who ate the fruit of the first tree died, and those who eat the flesh of the Son of God will live forever.

All who eat the Fruit of this dark and ugly tree will receive the antidote to the sweet, poisoned fruit from the beautiful tree. And there is a far greater mystery: all who suffer the effects of the beautiful tree will find their suffering transformed by the ugly tree. The weakness, failure, pain and trauma of humankind have been united to the Son of God on the ugly tree. Now, our brokenness is a thing of God, and through our brokenness we will triumph, by the grace of God. O happy fault, that earned so great, so glorious a Redeemer! Our triumph will be greater than the depth of our fall.

By a tree we were destroyed. Our Father tried to warn us. That tree would give us the knowledge of good and evil–because, to know evil, you have to experience evil. And our Father didn't wand us to experience evil. He wanted us to be happy. But we had to see for ourselves. Our Father told us that if evil came into the world, we would surely die, but we had to find out what that meant. So we did evil, and became evil, and evil came upon us, and Man became a thing that turned from God to a tree and died. Christ desired to be one with us, wherever we would go. So, with the Father's blessing, He left His Father's house. He came down from Heaven. He permitted evil to befall Himself, He embraced the tree, and He died.

That tree, long ago, was beautiful, green and covered in sweet fruits. The tree we see now is ugly– it bears no leaves or blossoms. Only one fruit hangs there, the fruit of our sin: the Son of God who loves us, disfigured, ruined, crying out in torment and giving up the Ghost. But those who ate the fruit of the first tree died, and those who eat the flesh of the Son of God will live forever.

All who eat the Fruit of this dark and ugly tree will

receive the antidote to the sweet, poisoned fruit from the beautiful tree. And there is a far greater mystery: all who suffer the effects of the beautiful tree will find their suffering transformed by the ugly tree. The weakness, failure, pain and trauma of humankind have been united to the Son of God on the ugly tree. Now, our brokenness is a thing of God, and through our brokenness we will triumph, by the grace of God. O happy fault, that earned so great, so glorious a Redeemer! Our triumph will be greater than the depth of our fall.

We will be with Him in Paradise.

You and I will be with Him in Paradise.

You, with all of your pain, your failure, your shame, your ugliness– you will be healed and brought to paradise. You will take your place as the bride of the Son of God. You will find that all of your sufferings have been traded for glory and beauty in paradise.

You are redeemed, by the sign of the ugly tree.

13

THE THIRTEENTH STATION: JESUS IS TAKEN DOWN FROM THE CROSS

*W*e adore You, O Christ, and we bless You, because by Your holy cross You have redeemed the world.

There were some women watching from a distance. Among them were Mary of Magdala, Mary who was the mother of James the younger and Joses, and Salome. These used to follow him and look after him when he was in Galilee. And there were many other women there who had come up to Jerusalem with him. It was now evening, and since it was Preparation Day (that is, the vigil of the sabbath), there came Joseph of Arimathea, a prominent member of the Council, who himself lived in the hope of seeing the kingdom of God, and he boldly went to Pilate and asked for the body of Jesus.

— MARK 15:40

It's over.

It's truly over.

Man has murdered God.

The faithless killed the One who remains faithful, in the most painful way they could devise.

He remained faithful until the very end.

He loved us with His last breath, but that's over now. And the faithless were surprised it took such a short time. They wanted to have more fun, but He suffocated in just about three hours. He was so weak —hardly worth their time.

They took Him down from the Cross, and they gave His body to His mother.

And now, what can we say?

We've seen this scene so many times. In each generation, there are people who are important and people who are not —aren't there? Everyone seems to accept that that's the case. There are citizens and slaves, civilized people and savages, colonists and natives, conquerors we're told are brave and conquered men we're told are cowards. There are people whose skin is the right color and people whose skin is wrong. There are people who speak the right language and people who are barbarians. There are those who matter, and those who don't. The important and the unimportant.

This is the way of the world.

When the unimportant get in the way of the important, they have to be gotten out of the way. Sometimes they have to be killed. Sometimes the important have to make that death as painful as possible in order to prove their point. Otherwise, more unimportant people would get in the way, and that would lead to more deaths. So they invent new and hideous ways to kill unimportant people. They're crucified, drawn and quartered, burned alive, lynched. Afterwards, their mothers come and collect the body, if there's anything left.

The mothers mourn, and no one can console them, but what should we do?

We have a law, and according to that law, He ought to be crucified. So we crucified Him. We incurred no guilt —did we? We only did what the world told us was necessary.

Now He is gone. His mother cradles His destroyed body, and mourns, and cannot be consoled.

What can we say to her?

She is not important.

This is the way of the world.

But Heaven has a different way.

When Heaven entered the world, He entered as an unimportant person. He entered as a poor manual laborer from a conquered nation. He entered as One Who would never count as valuable in the eyes of the world. The One Who is above the Cherubim chose an unimportant woman from an unimportant race, and saved her from all sin before she was created. He filled her with every grace, so that she could be the vessel of the Most High. Then He came to dwell in her, and through her He came to us. By her, he was raised in obscurity as an unimportant man. He went forth and preached the Gospel to the important and the unimportant alike —but in particular, he sought out the unimportant, the ones who don't matter, the ones who get in the way. He touched them, He healed them, He stayed at their houses. He even chose them for His priests.

This unimportant man got in the way, so important men did to Him what they have done from the beginning of time. They lynched Him. And when He was dead, they cut Him down. His mother held His body.

His mother mourned. The sky was dark. The temple veil was torn in two.

In all of eternity you will never find anyone holier, than this unimportant woman and her unimportant Son.

And in this way, the whole world is forever shamed. The spirit of the world is put to flight.

From this day until the end of time, the unimportant people who get in the way have become the icons of the Son of God and His most holy Mother.

14

THE FOURTEENTH STATION: JESUS
IS LAID IN THE TOMB

*W*e adore You, O Christ, and we praise You, because by Your holy cross You have redeemed the world.

When it was evening, there came a rich man from Arimathea, named Joseph, who was also a disciple of Jesus. He went to Pilate and asked for the body of Jesus; then Pilate ordered it to be given to him. So Joseph took the body and wrapped it in a clean linen cloth and laid it in his own new tomb, which he had hewn in the rock. He then rolled a great stone to the door of the tomb and went away. Mary Magdalene and the other Mary were there, sitting opposite the tomb.

The next day, that is, after the day of Preparation, the chief priests and the Pharisees gathered before Pilate and said,

Sir, we remember what that impostor said while he was still alive, 'After three days I will rise again.' Therefore command the tomb to be made secure until the third day; otherwise his disciples may go and steal him away, and tell the people, 'He has been raised from the dead,' and the last deception would be worse than the first.

Pilate said to them,

You have a guard of soldiers; go, make it as secure as you can.

So they went with the guard and made the tomb secure by sealing the stone.

— MATTHEW 27:57-66

Our Lord has passed from our sight.

He is gone from our sight.

While He was here, we didn't know Him. We saw a stranger; a foreigner; a nuisance; one who favored all the wrong people. We killed Him so He couldn't get in our way ever again, and now He is gone from our sight.

But the rulers of the world are still afraid. The Jews and the Gentiles conspired together to kill the Lord; now they conspire to keep Him dead. They find that they've accidentally fulfilled His prophecy of being crucified in Jerusalem; they don't want Him to rise again as He further prophesied, or even to appear to rise. They want to be sure He stays dead.

They set a guard on the tomb. Imagine —not just one guard but a complement of guards patrolling a fresh grave. It would be comical if it weren't so macabre. They publicly tortured Him to death, and now they've sent guards to a tomb to make sure He stays that way. He mustn't rise. He mustn't leave the tomb. No one can be allowed to hope that He will leave the tomb. No one can be allowed to make it look as though He's left. All hope must die from this minute. Everyone saw our sin; no one must see how God turns the sin into glory.

They failed in faith when they would not listen to Christ.

They failed in love when they killed Him. Now they attempt to bury all hope and keep it sealed in the tomb forever. If Christ rises from the dead then our hope is not lost, and faith and love can be brought to life again. They can't have that. It would ruin their plans.

Meanwhile, there are the two Marys —not the Mother of God but two less significant Marys sitting opposite the tomb. The guards don't bother to send them away. They're worthless: not only foreign women of a conquered race, but women of ill repute, below the notice of the Roman guards, at least when they are on duty.

Christ was born in a cave, in a village where His parents were because of Rome's decree. Now He is dead, in a cave, with guards patrolling His resting place because of Rome's decree. He spent His life caring for disreputable people of no significance; now only disreputable people of no significance are there to mourn.

His disciples are afraid, hiding in the upper room. Those who killed Him are also afraid —so afraid they send guards to patrol in front of the tomb, for fear that Christ could still win.

The women who did not abandon Him are in mourning, but they will be comforted.

This is how it stood on the Sabbath, the last day of the week, at the end of the Way of the Cross and the beginning of what happened next.

15

THE FIFTEENTH STATION: THE RESURRECTION

*W*e Adore You, O Christ, and we praise You, because by Your holy Cross You have redeemed the world.

After the Sabbath, at dawn on the first day of the week, Mary Magdalene and the other Mary went to look at the tomb.

There was a violent earthquake, for an angel of the Lord came down from heaven and, going to the tomb, rolled back the stone and sat on it. His appearance was like lightning, and his clothes were white as snow. The guards were so afraid of him that they shook and became like dead men.

The angel said to the women, "Do not be afraid, for I know that you are looking for Jesus, who was crucified. He is not here; he has risen, just as he said. Come and see the place where he lay. Then go quickly and tell his disciples: 'He has risen from the dead and is going ahead of you into Galilee. There you will see him.' Now I have told you."

So the women hurried away from the tomb, afraid yet filled with joy, and ran to tell his disciples. Suddenly Jesus met them. "Greetings," he said. They came to him, clasped his feet and worshiped him. Then Jesus said to them, "Do not be afraid. Go and tell my brothers to go to Galilee; there they will see me."

— MATTHEW 28:1-7

I can't tell you what happens next.

Or, at least, I can't tell you what happens next, in the same way that I told you what happened up to this point.

I have told you about how Christ suffered in order to be with you in suffering, and died in order to be with you in death. Suffering and death are things we understand. They happen every day. They are our things.

The Resurrection is how Christ began to take you up to where He is —and where God is, belongs to God.

Suffering and death are human things, and God became a human to share them with us. The Resurrection is where the God who became a human begins to draw humans up into God.

What does that look like?

A soul that descended into hell, returns to the Body it left.

Warmth returns to what was cold.

A heart that was still for days, beats.

A diaphragm moves, and the still air of the tomb rushes into lungs that were empty.

He stands, and walks out of the tomb.

It might have looked something like that.

We saw Him scourged, condemned, humiliated, stripped and raised up on the cross, but the moment of Resurrection is hidden from us. We saw God take up everything that is ours, but the moment when He begins to give us what is His, is hidden. All we see is what happened outside: the thunderclap, the appearance of the angel. The guards, the people who killed Him, become themselves like dead men, but the dead Man is not in the tomb.

The women who had sat opposite the tomb witnessed all of this; then they ran to tell the disciples, but on the way, they saw Him.

They saw Him alive, and so will you.

The day is coming when the moment of Resurrection will no longer be shrouded in mystery. It will happen to you and to me. Christ has taken on everything that humans have. Now He has already begun to give us everything that is His, and one day this work will be complete.

Christ has gone ahead of us to Galilee. Go quickly and tell the disciples that He is risen from the dead. While we are hurrying to tell the good news, He will come to us. He will find us and we will see that all of this is true.

A little further and we, ourselves, will be risen from the dead.

The wedding feast of the Lamb has begun, and you, the bride, go forth to welcome Him.

He has done all of this for you, and now He is doing something new.

Amen.

Made in the USA
Coppell, TX
08 June 2020

27358337R00035